Traditional Hymns

BOOK 2

Arranged by Fred Kern • Phillip Keveren • Mona Rejino

Range

Symbols

ppp, *pp*, *p*, *mp*, *mf*, *f*, *ff*, ♯, ♭, ♮,
rit., cresc., 8va, 15ma, legato, dim.,
a tempo, poco a poco, sempre, simile

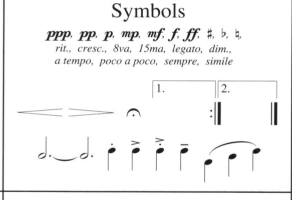

Rhythm

time signatures:
3/4, **4/4**, **6/8**, **3/8**, **¢**

swing eighths

Intervals

2nds–octave
Chords and Inversions

ISBN 978-1-4234-8090-7

HAL•LEONARD®
CORPORATION
7777 W. BLUEMOUND RD. P.O. BOX 13819 MILWAUKEE, WI 53213

In Australia contact:
Hal Leonard Australia Pty. Ltd.
4 Lentara Court
Cheltenham, Victoria, 3192 Australia
Email: ausadmin@halleonard.com.au

Visit Hal Leonard Online at
www.halleonard.com

Traditional Hymns

BOOK 2

Suggested Order of Study:

Lead On, O King Eternal

Dear Lord and Father of Mankind

All Things Bright and Beautiful

God of Grace and God of Glory

Ezekiel Saw the Wheel

God Will Take Care of You

Lord, I Want to Be a Christian

This Is My Father's World

Eternal Father, Strong to Save

Nobody Knows the Trouble I've Seen

Softly and Tenderly

Stand Up, Stand Up for Jesus

Swing Low, Sweet Chariot

Let the Lower Lights Be Burning

In the Garden

Full orchestral arrangements, included with this book on CD, may be used for both practice and performance. The enclosed audio CD is playable on any CD player. For Windows and Mac computer users, the CD is enhanced so you can access MIDI files for each song.

 TRACKS 9/10

The first track number is a practice tempo. The second track number is the performance tempo.

Contents

Lead On, O King Eternal

Words by Ernest W. Shurtleff
Music by Henry T. Smart
Arranged by Mona Rejino

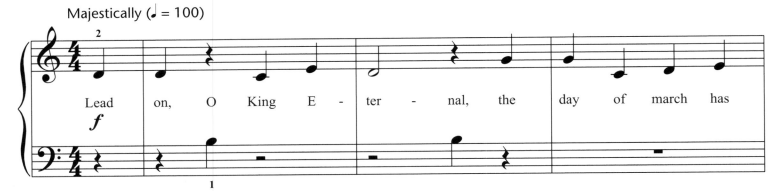

Lead on, O King E - ter - nal, the day of march has

come; hence - forth in fields of con - quest Thy

Accompaniment (Student plays one octave higher than written.) TRACKS 1/2

tents shall be our home.   Thro' days of prep - a -

mp

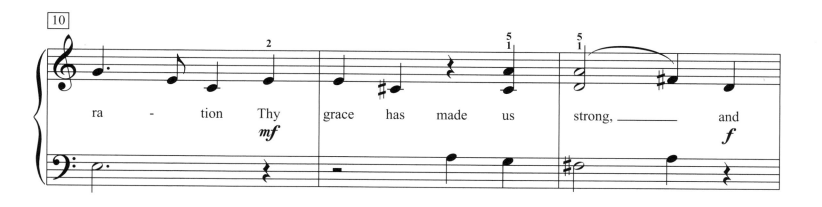

ra - tion Thy grace has made us strong, _____ and

mf   *f*

now, O King E - ter - nal, we lift our bat - tle song.

rit.

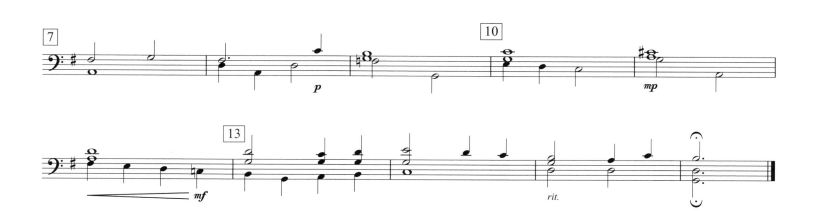

p   *mp*

mf   *rit.*

Dear Lord and Father of Mankind

Words by John Greenleaf Whittier
Music by Frederick Charles Maker
Arranged by Mona Rejino

God of Grace and God of Glory

Words by Harry Emerson Fosdick
Music by John Hughes
Arranged by Fred Kern

Joyfully (♩ = 96) TRACKS 5/6

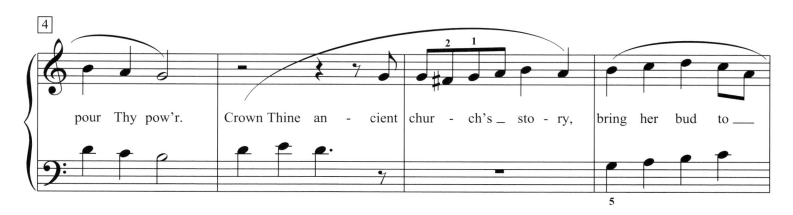

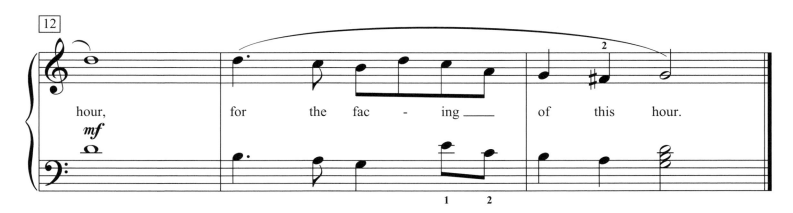

All Things Bright and Beautiful

Words by Cecil Frances Alexander
17th Century English Melody
Arranged by Mona Rejino

made their glow - ing ___ col - ors, He ___ made their ti - ny ___

cresc.

wings. All things bright and beau - ti - ful, all

mf

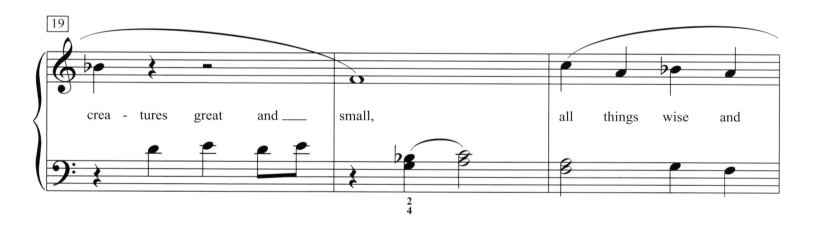

crea - tures great and ___ small, all things wise and

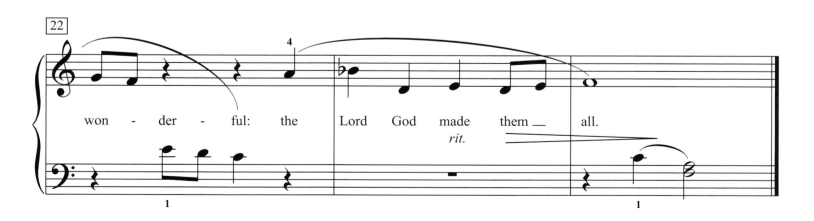

won - der - ful: the Lord God made them ___ all.

rit.

9

Ezekiel Saw the Wheel

Traditional Spiritual
Arranged by Phillip Keveren

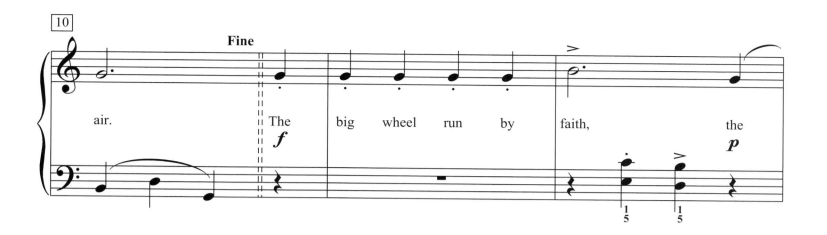

This Is My Father's World

Words by Maltbie D. Babcock
Music by Franklin L. Sheppard
Arranged by Mona Rejino

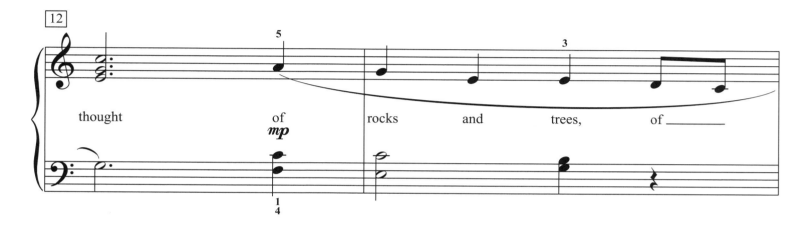

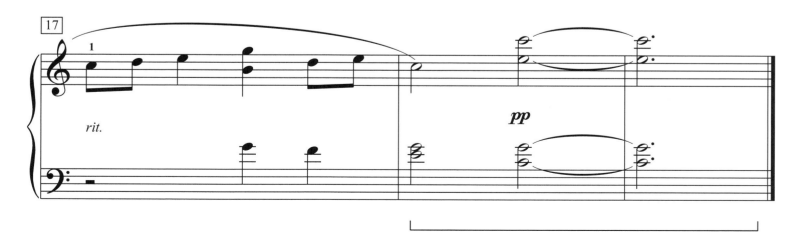

Lord, I Want to Be a Christian

Traditional Spiritual
Arranged by Mona Rejino

heart, in my heart, in my heart, in my heart. Lord, I

want to be a Chris-tian in my heart.

God Will Take Care of You

Words by Civilla D. Martin
Music by W. Stillman Martin
Arranged by Phillip Keveren

thro' ev - 'ry day, o'er all the way; He will take

care ___ of you, God will take care ___ of you.

Fine

Thro' days of toil ___ when heart doth fail, God will take care of you. ___

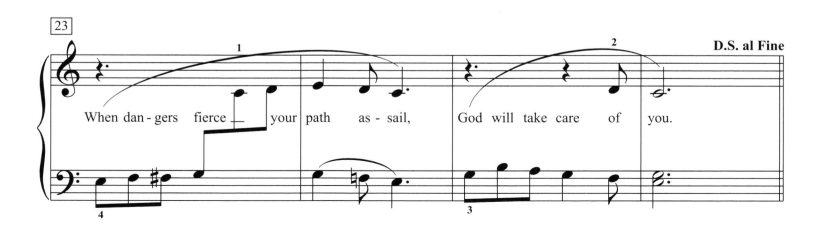

When dan - gers fierce ___ your path as - sail, God will take care of you.

D.S. al Fine

Eternal Father, Strong to Save

Words by William Whiting
Music by John Bacchus Dykes
Arranged by Phillip Keveren

Nobody Knows the Trouble I've Seen

African-American Spiritual
Arranged by Phillip Keveren

to the ground, _ Oh, yes, Lord! No - bod - y knows the
trou - ble I've seen, no - bod - y knows but Je - sus; _____
no - bod - y knows the trou - ble I've seen, glo - ry, hal - le -
lu - jah! Glo - ry, hal - le - lu - jah!

Softly and Tenderly

Words and Music by Will L. Thompson
Arranged by Phillip Keveren

watch - ing, watch - ing for you and for me. _____ Come

home, _____ come home, _____ you who are wea - ry, come

home. _____ Ear - nest - ly, ten - der - ly, Je - sus is

call - ing, call - ing, O sin - ner, come home!

Swing Low, Sweet Chariot

Traditional Spiritual
Arranged by Mona Rejino

looked o - ver Jor - dan, and what did I see, ___ com - ing for to car - ry me

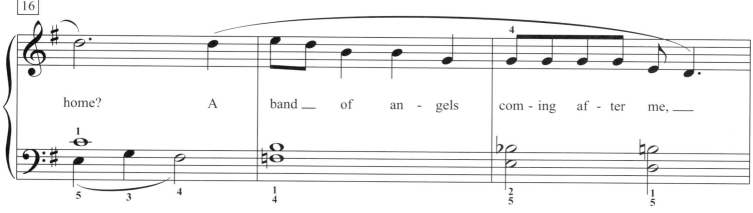

home? A band ___ of an - gels com - ing af - ter me, ___

D.S. al Coda

CODA

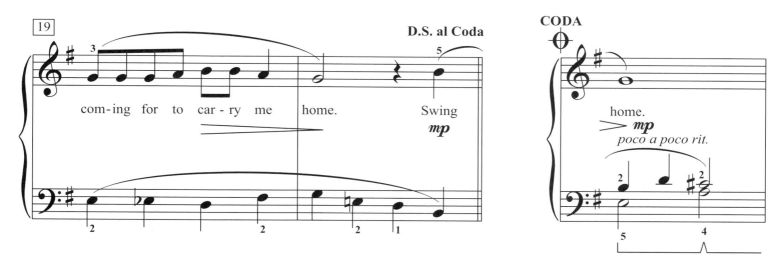

com - ing for to car - ry me home. Swing *mp*

home. *mp* *poco a poco rit.*

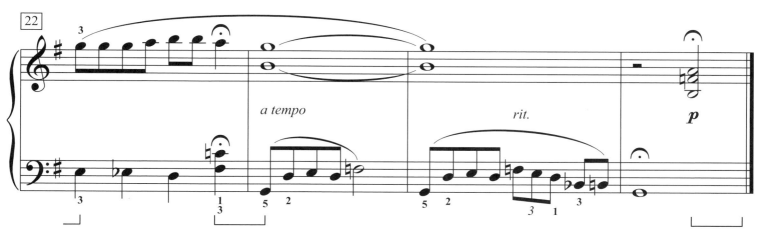

a tempo *rit.* *p*

In the Garden

Words and Music by
C. Austin Miles
Arranged by Phillip Keveren

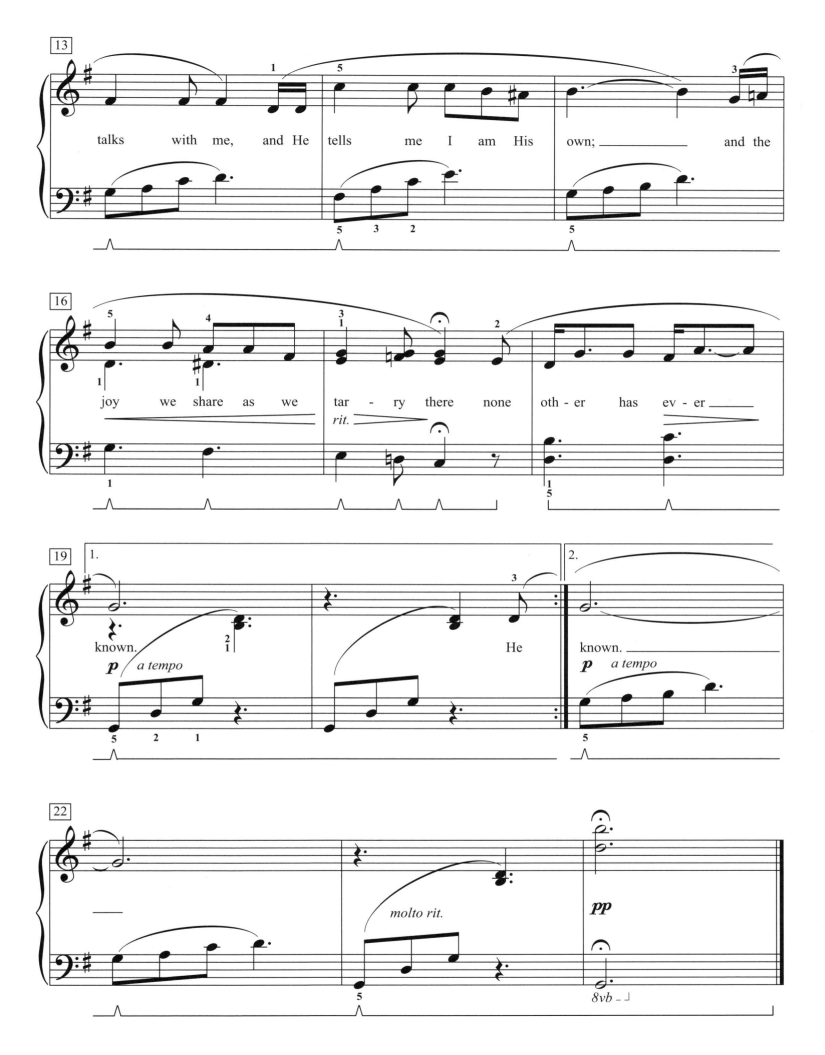

talks with me, and He tells me I am His own; _____ and the joy we share as we tar - ry there none oth - er has ev - er _____

rit.

1. known. *p* *a tempo*

He known. _____ *p* *a tempo*

molto rit.

pp

8vb

27

Stand Up, Stand Up for Jesus

Words by George Duffield, Jr.
Music by George J. Webb
Arranged by Fred Kern

Lyrics under the staves:

lead, _____ till ev - 'ry foe is van - quished, and
be; _____ He with the King of Glo - ry and shall

Christ is Lord in - deed. Stand
reign e - ter - nal -

ly.

Let the Lower Lights Be Burning

Words and Music by
Philip P. Bliss
Arranged by Fred Kern

Hal Leonard Student Piano Library

Adult Piano Method

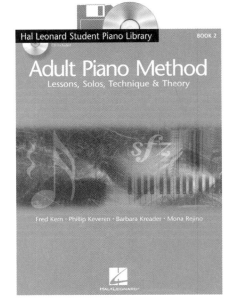

Adult Piano Method

Adults want to play rewarding music and enjoy their piano study. They deserve a method that lives up to those expectations. The new *Hal Leonard Student Piano Library Adult Piano Method* does just that and more.

Method Book 1
00296441 Book/CD..$16.95
00296442 Book/GM Disk...$16.95

Method Book 2
00296480 Book/CD..$16.95
00296481 Book/GM Disk...$16.95

Popular Hits Book 1

Our hit-packed supplementary songbook includes these titles: American Pie • Circle of Life • Fun, Fun, Fun • Let It Be Me • Murder, She Wrote • The Music of the Night • My Heart Will Go On • Sing • Strangers in the Night • Vincent (Starry Starry Night) • Y.M.C.A. • The Way You Look Tonight.

00296541 Book/CD..$12.95
00296542 Book/GM Disk...$12.95

Popular Hits Book 2

12 hits: I Will Remember You • I Wish You Love • I Write the Songs • In the Mood • Moon River • Oh, Pretty Woman • The Phantom of the Opera • Stand by Me • Tears in Heaven • Unchained Melody • What a Wonderful World • When I'm Sixty-Four.

00296652 Book/CD..$12.95
00296653 Book/GM Disk...$12.95

Christmas Favorites Book 1

12 favorites: Away in a Manger • Deck the Hall • God Rest Ye Merry, Gentlemen • I Saw Three Ships • Jingle Bells • Joy to the World • O Come, O Come, Emmanuel • O Little Town of Bethleham • Silent Night • Ukrainian Bell Carol • We Wish You a Merry Christmas • What Child Is This?

00296544 Book/CD Pack..$12.95
00296547 Book/GM Disk...$12.95

Christmas Favorites Book 2

12 more holiday classics: Angels We Have Heard on High • Bring a Torch, Jeannette Isabella • Dance of the Sugar Plum Fairy • Ding Dong! Merrily on High! • The First Noel • Go, Tell It on the Mountain • Hark! The Herald Angels Sing • The Holly and the Ivy • O Christmas Tree • O Holy Night • Still, Still, Still • We Three Kings of Orient Are.

00296668 Book/CD Pack..$12.95
00296669 Book/GM Disk...$12.95

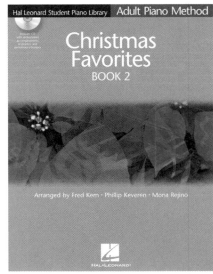

0706